SEE YOU SOON!

A Story of Hope from the
Life of Danielle Grace

WRITTEN BY DR. DANIEL R. CARFREY

ARPress
ILLUMINATING IDEAS.
EMPOWERING VOICES

ARPress
45 Dan Road Suite 36
Canton MA 02021

| Hotline: | 1(888) 821-0229 |
| Fax: | 1(508) 545-7580 |

Ordering Information:
Quantity Sales. Special discounts are available on quantity purchases by corporations, associations, and others. For details, contact the publisher at the address above.

Printed in the United States of America.

| ISBN-13 | Paperback | 979-8-89356-585-0 |
| | eBook | 979-8-89356-586-7 |

Library of Congress Control Number: 2024903091

Acknowledgements

We would like to extend special thanks to:

Our parents, who stood beside us, prayed for us, and lifted us up so many times.

Dr. Jill Gaines, for her exemplary care and support throughout both pregnancies.

Terri Goad and the nursing staff on the maternity floor, for their extra care during MarySusan's recovery, as well as the "memory box" they created for us.

Mary Wall, for helping us capture priceless moments with Danielle through photography that we will hold on to for the rest of our lives.

Pastor Robert Alderman, for his encouragement and for officiating Danielle's graveside service.

Countless family and friends who loved, encouraged, and took care of us in more ways than we can list.

TABLE OF CONTENTS

PREFACE

"**D**r. Carfrey, I want a copy of that book as soon as it is published." This has been the comment I have heard many times since I began telling people I intended to write about the experience of losing our granddaughter, Danielle Grace, when she was just twenty-two weeks old. That was almost a year ago. In looking back upon my years of ministry, I do not think that I have been as sensitive as perhaps I should have been, to what women experience in losing their child while still in the womb, or at the time of birth.

That has dramatically changed for me.

It is for that reason I have written this book, sharing the deep feelings my wife Shirley and I felt as we went through this experience with our daughter, MarySusan. This book also includes in their own words, some of the reflections that she and her husband; our son-in-law Brandon, had at the time. I am glad to say that we all have come through this experience with an even stronger faith in our Lord Jesus Christ and the plan of God for our lives. It is His grace and peace that has sustained us, as you too will experience, if you have personally called upon the name of Jesus to be your personal Savior.

This book not only shares our experience with you, the reader, but shares as well why we strongly believe that we will see Danielle Grace again. We also include some help from the Bible as to how any believer can, with the help of the Lord, handle great grief and negative emotions in the loss of a loved one.

If you have any questions or words of encouragment for us as a result of reading this book, we would love to hear from you. Dr. Dan Carfrey, c/o Appalachian Bible College, 161 College Drive, Mt. Hope WV, 25880. If you would like to keep up with the ongoing story of my daughter and son-in-law.

CHAPTER ONE
ABOUT DANI'S PARENTS

MarySusan Williams was herself, a gift from the Lord. Shirley Caudill and I, Dan Carfrey, were married in a little country church in eastern Kentucky where I had been a pastor. I had decided to join the Army as a Chaplain's Assistant, and we relocated to Columbia, South Carolina where I reported for duty at Fort Jackson in June of 1973.

The Joy and Sorrow

It wasn't long before my wife became pregnant. She was only fourteen weeks into her pregnancy when she miscarried, due to a robbery at the bank where she worked. How does one explain this? The doctors told us that there was probably something wrong to begin with, for the miscarriage to occur so easily. We counted the matter as being the Lord's will, and looked forward to the next time Shirley would become pregnant.

The Joy

It would be another ten years before my wife would become pregnant again; and this only after surgery in which we were told that even then, she would only have a twenty-five percent chance of conceiving. That's when God gave us a precious daughter in September of 1983. We named her after her mother and my stepmother, both of whose names were Mary. Susan was Shirley's youngest sister--who as a child born with Down Syndrome--had always had a special place in my wife's heart.

We celebrated her miracle birth with the words of Hannah as God answered her prayer for her son, Samuel. That was the verse my wife and I used and distributed with gold print on red book markers when MarySusan was born. *"For this child I prayed; and the LORD hath given me my petition, which I asked of him."* (1 Samuel 1:27) We felt that was far more appropriate than distributing cigars, as was the common practice in that day.

We didn't want her to be called just Mary, and people forget her middle name. So we combined the two names without separating them, and by capitalizing the "S" in the name Susan to indicate both as being equally important. Thus she was named "MarySusan" and she has been a source of joy to our hearts from the time of her birth; not only because she was pretty outwardly, but she was beautiful on the inside. She accepted the Lord Jesus as her personal Savior at a very early age, and demonstrated her Christian faith in so many ways while growing up.

MarySusan met Brandon as they entered studies at Appalachian Bible College in Bradley, West Virginia in the fall of 2001. I was driving on the campus when I noticed my daughter in the company of Brandon. I looked at my wife and asked, "Who is that boy?!" Well, that "boy" became our son-in-law. They became husband and wife in August of 2005.

CHAPTER TWO
JOY TURNED INTO SORROW

In MarySusan's First Pregnancy

The Joy

All of MarySusan's life she had wanted to be a mother. Although she had demonstrated a special gift in teaching elementary students, she longed to have a child of her own. I will never forget the joy we had when they shared with us that she was pregnant. The Sorrow

Yet a very rare event happened. Not only would the baby not survive, but MarySusan's life was also in jeopardy. I will never forget the pain on our daughter's face when her doctor came in to take her to surgery. Nor will I forget our emotional pain for our daughter, knowing MarySusan herself could die on the operating table. It seemed like an eternity as we waited to hear the results. But in answer to our prayers, not only did MarySusan come through the surgery fine, but would be able to conceive again--if the Lord so willed.

In MarySusan's Second Pregnancy

The Joy

It was three years later that MarySusan conceived again. How thrilled we were. We had prayed continuously that God would enable her to do so, knowing how much she wanted to be a mother.

She would call us every day for the next twenty-two weeks, sharing with us her joy. One day, I asked her if she could feel her daughter move yet and she said that in church that evening she had looked down and saw her stomach move. She giggled, and I laughed. I said, "MarySusan, I am so thrilled for you that the Lord is giving you an experience we men would never want to have." She giggled some more.

Thank you, Lord, for answering our prayers.

The Sorrow

Emergency Surgery

On the morning of February 24, 2014, MarySusan woke up not feeling well. Brandon went to work, but came back to their house during his lunch break to check on her. She had been vomiting and was in intense pain. Brandon rushed her to her doctor, who then admitted her to the hospital. I had prayed for both of them early that morning, and I believe God put it into Brandon's mind and heart to go check on MarySusan.

When they arrived at the hospital, it did not take them long to determine the emergency of the situation.

They began preparing her for surgery right away. I was in Beckley, West Virginia, going over a lesson with a man in our church. I was reviewing with him a lesson I had written and had shared many times with students at Appalachian Bible College regarding negative emotions, and how to handle them God's way. Talk about the need for a preacher to apply what he teaches to others! While I was going over this lesson with the man, my wife called to inform me that they were rushing my daughter to surgery.

We immediately prepared to leave Beckley for Roanoke, VA, where Brandon and MarySusan lived. It was 7:30 in the evening, and it was a two hour drive. On the way, I prayed out loud to the Lord to have mercy on both my daughter and the baby. We felt so helpless, knowing that the surgery was taking place even as we were on the road. But I trusted in the goodness of our God who had been so good to Shirley and I down through the years.

Emotional Trauma

I was unable to reach Brandon's father; Les, as we got close to Roanoke. I told my wife that he might be talking with the doctors at that very moment as to the outcome of the surgery. When we arrived, several of Brandon and MarySusan's pastors were there with Brandon's family. Les informed us that the outcome had not been good. MarySusan had lost her baby. Our hearts felt the pain and immediate sorrow and I asked, "Is MarySusan alive?" To my relief, the answer was "Yes." Thank you, Lord.

But then, we experienced another negative strike to our hearts. We were given more information as to what had happened. As MarySusan describes in the next chapter, what happened on the operating table showed God's hand and His perfect timing.

So again, we felt both joy and sorrow; joy in her life being spared, and yet sorrow, knowing that our daughter would never be able to conceive again. It seemed that we waited a long time for Brandon, along with the doctors, to inform MarySusan as to the outcome of her surgery. Afterwards, MarySusan called for Shirley and I to come in. She wept as she informed me of the name she and Brandon had selected beforehand; Danielle Grace, "Dani Grace" as the shortened version. We wept with her.

She asked me to read her some Scripture. In the rush to get there, I had left my Bible in the parking lot of the hospital, so I began quoting some memorized Scriptures from the book of Psalms. I asked her if that helped, and she smiled in agreement.

Emotional Bonding

The next morning, the nurses brought in Danielle for MarySusan and Brandon to hold for the first time. When Shirley and I were invited to join them, I could not believe my eyes the first time I saw her. What a beautiful child! How precious it was to see my daughter smiling down upon her. We laughed and cried together as we each held her in our arms, noting the physical characteristics each of us saw that resembled (in our eyes) one or more of us. She was so tiny, and yet the formation of the body the Lord had prepared for her seemed so intricate, so precise, down to the little fingers and toes.

We all shared the joy together; Shirley and I, as well as Les and Jean, Brandon's parents. We took lots of pictures together. MarySusan told her mother privately:

"Mommy, now I know what it is like to feel a mother's love. I have never experienced such love before." When Shirley told me later what MarySusan had said, I whispered the words in my heart again; "Thank you, Lord." The love my wife and I experienced as grandparents for this little girl was placed in our hearts by the Lord who gave her to us.

The times for grief would come often. But there would be joy in the midst of sorrow. The need for continual prayer remained for all of us. How gracious God's people were in conveying multiple expressions of their prayers for us during this time; by way of personal visits to the hospital, through Facebook, email, and text messages. As the words of the chorus say; "*I'm so glad I'm a part of the family of God.*" We rejoiced that our daughter and son-in-law were so well liked.

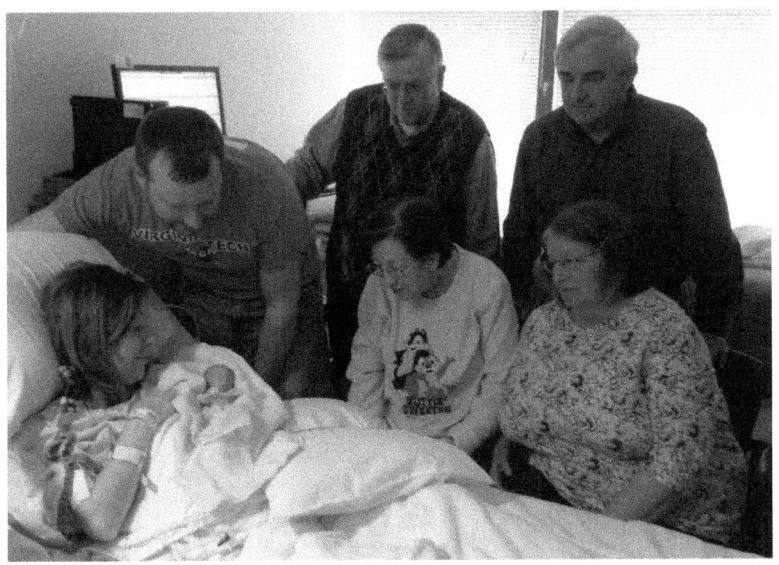

Both sets of Grandparents: Dan and Shirley Carfrey (nearest to MarySusan and Brandon, and Les and Jean Williams

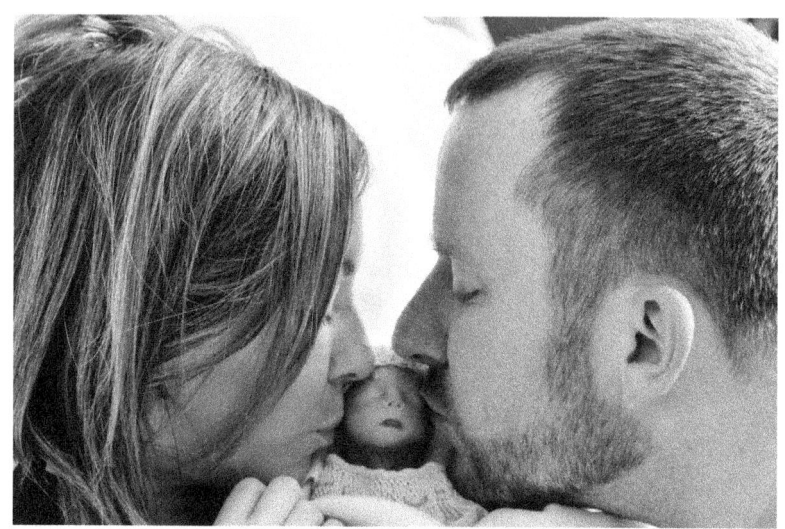

MarySusan and Brandon embracing Danielle

CHAPTER THREE
IN THEIR OWN WORDS

MarySusan's Personal Testimony

My First Pregnancy

For as long as I can remember I have wanted to be a mother. Most kids have imaginary friends when they are little, but I had imaginary children. Five children; to be exact. As an only child; I had to occupy my time somehow! I chose a career mostly because it was expected. Yes; I do think God called me to teach (and I do love it), but my true heart's desire has simply been to raise my own children.

It has been a long, long road. It took almost a year of trying before we became pregnant. We found out that we were expecting our first child right before our 5th anniversary in August of 2010. We had been through a lot that year already, and this child seemed to be a sign of God's favor. I would only carry Baby #1 for 9 weeks before we lost him or her in a very rare situation that only 2% of women have ever experienced. God was still showing us that He was in control, though.

The surgery planned was a dangerous, extensive one. At the last moment, my doctor decided to try a less invasive route, even though the chances were slim that it would be successful. The procedure worked, and as a result; I would still be able to carry a child in the future!

Someone once said that one does not ever get over the loss of a child; I have found this to be very true. Even months later; I would still come home from teaching school and cry because I had no baby to hold. There was a sense of emptiness. Still, there was the hope of the future. After we lost the first baby, my desire for a child only intensified. We were unable to get pregnant after losing our first baby, so I began to go through fertility testing and treatments. After about eight months, I was finally put in contact with a specialist in another city who recognized immediately that I had extensive damage from the surgery in 2010.

Two other surgeries, some very painful testing, months of treatments, emotional ups and downs, plus thousands of dollars later, we found out we were expecting our "rainbow" baby. (When you have a baby after losing one, it is called a "rainbow" baby.) When I first learned of this reference, I thought it was perfect. There were three separate times on this journey that I had asked God to remind me He was there and that everything would be okay, and all three times He had shown me a rainbow.

My Second Pregnancy with Dani Grace

I had called out to God for years, seeking to trust Him, and learning how to ask with belief and expectation. It had been three years and one month since we had lost our first child. We had always felt that God would redeem our story and allow us to have a second opportunity. Especially because of the way He had worked in the surgery of 2010, allowing me to be able to carry again. Those years of having to battle emotions; avoid baby showers, nurseries, and dealing with an answer of "No," had come to an end. Finally.

"Thankful" does not begin to describe our overwhelming sense of gratitude for this gift. We immediately told family and close friends. Within a couple of weeks, we decided to announce it, because we knew the importance of having others to begin praying for this child. People were ecstatic for us. We were told we were an "inspiration" because we held on to hope when it seemed we should have given up. Even my doctor, who had been on this journey with us since 2010, was absolutely thrilled for us. I used to literally feel sick if I had to go to visit the building where her office was located, but now it would represent a place of dreams fulfilled, instead of dreams dashed.

Fear was something I would battle from day one in this pregnancy. I never had the luxury of assuming things would go well in my pregnancies. I began to fight these fears, and I mean really fight them. Through Scripture and prayer, God began to help me rest in Him over the future of this baby. I would remind myself out loud sometimes that this was not our child, but His. I knew that He wanted me to trust Him and I reached the point that my trust in God outweighed my fears. I experienced Psalm 34:4; "I sought the LORD, and He heard me, and delivered me from all my fears."

While we were going to be happy either way, Brandon was convinced our baby was a boy. But I wasn't so sure. I hadn't experienced a lot of morning sickness, and that went along with the wives' tales we had heard. Still, my mom thought it was a girl, and she was right! When Brandon and I found out the baby's gender, we were surprised, but we fell in love with our child even more. We had mostly decided on a name, even though Brandon wasn't ready to fully commit yet! We told everyone it was a girl, but didn't reveal her name. I wanted that to be our secret to treasure since we had told everyone immediately that we were expecting.

We had many ultrasounds, and I was monitored closely because of my history. Each ultrasound looked great, our baby was strong, and my doctor told me I appeared to be having a "normal" pregnancy. What?! I had never had anything go "normally" for me! My friends started talking about the showers they wanted to throw me, and I decided I wanted a rainbow shower to go with my rainbow baby. Brandon and I loved to go shopping; buying cute "monkey" outfits when we would find a sale (we had already nicknamed her our "Little Monkey"). The stores and aisles I had once avoided were now our Saturday destinations. I decided on colors for the nursery and we began to literally pile things in the spare room of our house with the intention of clearing out the guest room to become our baby's nursery. It would once again be used for what I had claimed it as in my mind years ago: a nursery.

At 20 weeks, I finally began to feel movement. I was sitting in church one night, and looked down to see my shirt move. I got so excited that I almost jumped up right in the middle of the sermon! Over the next week I got used to feeling her kick me. Brandon would try to feel the movement, but our baby would calm down as soon as he put his hand on my stomach. He wouldn't ever get the opportunity that most dads do to feel her moving around. My doctor said that I was feeling her move so late in my pregnancy due to the position of the placenta on the front of the uterus. Little did any of us know how much damage the placenta would actually cause.

Emergency Surgery Again

February 23, 2014. My last day to carry our baby girl. It was a Sunday, and I had immensely enjoyed singing in the choir at church that day. I loved to sing, but especially now that my little girl could recognize my voice. She would let me know she was there after we were finished singing and I sat down. That night I felt her moving, and again, Brandon tried to feel her too. She must have loved his hand and him talking to her because she calmed down again. About 3:00 a.m., February 24th; I got up feeling sick. After vomiting; my stomach muscles pulled and ached. This had happened once before and I was getting more sensitive to various foods, so I lay down and waited for the aching to go away. I wasn't too worried.

I didn't get much sleep that night so I decided to call in sick to work and take the day off for the first time since I had been pregnant. Brandon went to work, and I tried to get some sleep. When he came home around lunchtime to check on me, I was in so much pain I could hardly move. He looked at me and told me to call the doctor. I would find out later that I looked so white that it had moved him to action. My doctor was not there, and neither was her nurse; so I talked to someone else, who just recommended that I wait and try to hydrate myself.

When you are in the midst of a crisis, sometimes you don't see how God leads. Looking back, if He hadn't led us to decide to go to the doctor anyway, regardless of the nurse's advice, I would not be here today. Brandon had to help me to the car, with my pillow, towel, and trash can close by. By this point I felt delirious and nauseous. I could hardly walk into the office. The nurses immediately put me in a wheel chair, but when the nurse Practitioner saw me, she said we needed to go the ER to get fluids right away.

Having been through the ER experience several times before, and hoping to expedite the process, we asked her to call ahead and prepare them that we were coming. She did, and to my surprise, I was taken up to the maternity floor. They tried to get an IV going but couldn't, because my veins were closing up. A wonderful nurse came in to attempt the IV, and she would end up staying with me the rest of the afternoon and night. She was successful, but only after using a baby-size IV needle. The doctor on call and nurses all thought up to this point that I was just severely dehydrated and after some fluids, I should be good to go home. My veins were collapsing, but not from dehydration. When the blood work came back, it revealed that my platelet levels were severely low. Thankfully, our girl was still doing okay.

They transferred me to a room and did yet another ultrasound. I knew they were looking for something so I started to get a bit worried. My blood pressure was dangerously low so they tilted the angle of the bed so my head was down. Just lying there was so painful, and every time they touched me it seemed unbearable. The doctor told me I was having contractions. "No wonder

I am in pain," I thought. But this made me even more concerned for Baby Girl, as we lovingly called her now.

The doctor told me I was obviously bleeding internally and that they needed to do a CT scan to determine the location. She left, but came back soon after and told me she was afraid to wait to do a scan. I would need surgery immediately. She was hopeful that they could take care of it without disturbing our baby. She was friends with my personal doctor and said she would let her know. Another way that God was taking care of us.

We were told that because I was 22 weeks and 2 days; Baby Girl was just short of what they considered "viable" and they would not do anything to help her if she was delivered during the surgery. Up until this point, the gravity of the situation hadn't really hit me. I was getting more delirious all the time from loss of blood. But even in that state, I became irate. How could they refuse to help my baby if she needed it? They called in the head of the NICU to talk with us...to try to help calm me down, I'm sure. It's funny how some moments like those stick out in my mind, though much of it is a blur.

I told Brandon to call my parents, and they took me down to get ready for surgery. I remember the male doctor (who had been called in to help perform my surgery) telling Brandon that my body was in shock, and he couldn't express enough how serious this situation was. All the while, even though I was quite "out of it," I was very aware of the intense pain in my abdomen.

Once in the OR, they were trying to get me to move from the bed to the table, and I couldn't. Not that I didn't try, but I was in so much pain I absolutely could not move. The nurse, who had been by my side since inserting the IV, stepped in and said; "She can't. She is in too much pain." I was so thankful for her. She told me she would stay right with me during the surgery, and she did. When our baby girl entered this world, she was the one who immediately checked for a heartbeat, but there was none. She was also the one who took our daughter to Brandon for the first time. We know that God placed this lady there for our comfort that day and in the following week.

God had answered an unspoken prayer from me. I hadn't even known to pray this way, but He knew my mother's heart and answered anyway. God knew the horrible distress that I had felt in considering the possibility that my child would be born, struggling to survive, and not be given any medical help. So He took my child in His arms in a more peaceful way. While I was "still holding her inside," as my doctor says.

Post-Surgery Trauma

When one "wakes up" from surgery, it is not in a truly coherent state of mind. So when I woke up, I remember asking the nurse if my baby was okay. She just asked if I was ready to see my family. I knew the answer then. The rest of that night and even the following day are quite foggy in my memory. Most of what I know about it comes from what I have been told. One thing does remain in my mind though. That is when Brandon told me that he had given the official name of our baby to everyone. Danielle Grace. This was the name I had wanted so badly. But we had not fully committed to it yet. Danielle. The name I was almost given. And

Grace. Which Brandon chose, meaning "Blessing." I remember my heart soaring over this news.

My doctor, the one who had been with us through our journey, had come to be there for the surgery as well. She was off that day, but when she heard what was happening, she immediately came to the hospital. Her presence brought comfort when I woke up. God had blessed us with not just a doctor, but a friend. She would talk us through some of our most difficult days in the weeks to come.

The male doctor came in the next day and explained the details of what had completely shattered our world. The placenta had grown entirely through the wall of the uterus, wrapped around the outside, and then torn apart. They had removed over 2 liters of blood from my abdomen, causing my platelet level to dip into an extremely dangerous range. I had basically lost my blood supply. While I was on the operating table, my uterus had ruptured due to the attachment of the placenta on the outside of it. Had that not happened while I was already in surgery, the doctors would not have been able to get me to an operating room in time to save me. In other words, if I had gone into surgery just twenty minutes later, I would not have made it. Obviously, God's hand was in the timing.

I wouldn't be able to carry a baby again. This would prove to be something I would need to grieve as well. I had a vertical incision requiring almost forty staples to close up and a port in my neck that they had used to send blood directly to my heart. I would spend a week in the hospital while they watched my blood levels closely. There was also a scare of pneumonia, causing incredibly painful coughing.

During this week, we had many visitors from family and friends, but the only times I felt true peace were when I had Danielle in my arms. Even though I knew she was already in heaven, having her next to me made the pain easier to bear. I could honestly say that holding her made all the pain, money, and ups and downs worth it. The physical challenges of that week were many, and at times they overshadowed the emotional pain. There were a lot of tears in the hospital, but I was on some heavy doses of pain medicine, and it masked the reality a little for me.

We had a friend come take pictures of our sweet baby. The only pictures we would have of her. It was amazing how Dani Grace already had our features: my nose, Brandon's feet… she was absolutely perfect. We have some wonderful pictures of her to cherish.

Funeral Arrangements

We would need to make burial arrangements before leaving the hospital. Most parents have to give the name of a pediatrician, but we had to give the name of a funeral home. My brain literally could not handle making any decisions about this. In the following several weeks, the ability to make a decision (even about what to eat or how I wanted my pillow arranged) completely overwhelmed me to the point that I felt like my brain was shutting down. The trauma to my body and emotions affected me in surprising ways.

We had spent the week on the maternity floor. I didn't realize what Brandon had had to walk past every time he went down the hallway, until they made me leave my room to begin walking again. There were pictures of babies everywhere. On the walls. On the doors. Was this some form of cruel and unusual torture? Couldn't they understand what this would do to my emotions?

When it was time for me to be discharged from the hospital, a sweet nurse brought in our keepsake box. It was a beautiful, special box that they reserve only for unique situations. In it were Danielle's footprints and hand prints, her blanket, the tape measure used to measure her big feet and the wreath that had hung on the door alerting people to our situation. Nurses cried with us as we went down the hall. Our situation had affected others, too. I hung on to this beautiful, satin box all the way home. I would have dared anyone to try to pry it out of my hands. Leaving the hospital was one of the hardest things I had done thus far in my thirty years. I felt like I was leaving my baby, and it tore me apart.

The next morning (Sunday) we had to go to pick out a burial spot. It was so painful to get up and get dressed. I sat in the recliner, staring at one of the many floral arrangements sent to us by those who cared. I didn't really see it or anything else in the room. I felt empty. Heartless. I felt a darkness that I had never experienced in my whole life. It was from deep inside, and I felt like I was going down into a pit. It should have scared me to death, but I was grieving too much to feel fear. Looking back on it, it was really an evil feeling that I never want to experience again. I texted two close friends and told them what we had to do that day. I told them I needed prayer. I had no intention of praying myself (something very uncharacteristic of me), but I knew enough to know that I needed someone else to pray for me.

When we got to the cemetery, the man did not show up. That meant I had to go through this all over again tomorrow. That thought alone made me want to fall apart. There was another cemetery nearby that Brandon had driven through earlier that week, and we decided to go look at it. While we were in the car, I asked Brandon if he was glad I was still here. After all, medically speaking, I really shouldn't have made it. Of course, he said "yes" and looked at me with a puzzled expression on his face.

I cried and told him that I needed him to keep telling me over and over that he was glad I was here. Because I simply wasn't. I didn't want to be on this Earth. I wanted to be with my little girl. The one I had spent every second of over 22 weeks with. I did not think it was fair at all that God had taken her and left me here. This thought haunted me for the next several weeks and would be the source of much hurt that I would endure. Even in saying the words, I felt ashamed of myself. Life...God's greatest gift, and I wasn't thankful for it.

We liked the cemetery. As much as you can like a cemetery that you are choosing to bury your daughter in. There were trees. It was quiet and well-kept. We decided it was actually a good thing that the man at the first cemetery hadn't shown up.

The next day, we went to the funeral home and the new cemetery. It was snowing. For the first time in my life, I hated the snow. Its coldness matched the coldness I felt in my heart. The men who helped us at the funeral home and the cemetery were both so gentle. We picked a plot, but I couldn't handle picking out a marker for her grave as well, so we put that decision on hold. I couldn't even decide what I wanted to drink, much less what would stay permanently on my little girl's grave marker.

That night, I completely fell apart emotionally, telling Brandon that maybe, just maybe, I could have handled either the physical OR the emotional strain, but I absolutely could not do both at the same time. My breath was short and I felt as if I were having a panic attack.

Wednesday, March 5th. It was a beautiful day, but this is the day in which I would bury the body of my daughter. We had chosen to have a private family time at the funeral home, as well as a private graveside service. Some family members had travelled in, as well as a couple of close friends. Our doctor, who had become such a huge support, came as well. Danielle looked so sweet in a beautiful purple dress and a light pink hat, both made and given by friends. We placed a purple blanket over her and put a little monkey in the tiny coffin next to her. I arranged a tiny pink rose in her hand and we placed a floral arrangement on top of the coffin. We kissed her nose and said; "See you soon." That was the one thought I could cling to. I would see her again.

Flowers had been sent from a sweet friend and the choir/orchestra at church. Our best friends (who were in another country), made a rangoli; a memorial, to celebrate her life. Brandon, Danielle and I were being remembered by many friends, even though they were not there.

We chose to transport Danielle to the graveside in our car. It was the only time the three of us would travel together. Our pastor gave some encouraging words at the funeral, though admittedly, I couldn't listen very well. I tried to unglue my eyes from her coffin, right in front of me, but I couldn't. After the message, we chose to release a white dove while my dad led everyone in singing "Turn Your Eyes Upon Jesus." (This song had been special to me in high school.)

I couldn't sing. But I listened to Brandon's voice, marveling that it was so strong, and watched the dove fly away until I could see it no more. A strange peace came over me. The peace that I was used to feeling in my life. Not the evil. God gave me grace physically, emotionally, and spiritually that day. That evening, our families came over to eat with us. While everyone was talking, Brandon quietly told me that I should go look outside. Surrounding our house were many friends from the choir, orchestra, and our Sunday School class. They were praying for us. They had held a special prayer service the day after my surgery, and they were praying again. Then they sang; "Great is Thy Faithfulness." This was the most beautiful display of the body of Christ that I have ever seen. It lifted my sad heart.

The Days That Followed

The days that followed were full of much pain. The physical pain was great, and it was so difficult to even get up from a sitting position. I found that this directly affected my mental state of mind. I couldn't sleep either, and lack of sleep affects me even during normal times. If I felt really bad physically, I didn't feel like engaging in conversation or trying to do anything. I wanted to just sit there, completely succumbing to depression. This would in turn, affect my emotions. (Tears have never come in such a steady stream before as they do now.) My emotions ranged from sadness to depression to anger to hurt. I felt as if God, who had finally answered my prayers for a child, had betrayed me. Why would

He answer by giving me Danielle, only to take her away from me?

Sundays became so hard. I couldn't sing at church. The songs, full of God's promises, felt like they were hypocritical, empty words. Maybe they applied to other people, but not me. Not anymore. That only compounded my hurt. I felt like God had "let me down." I knew in my mind that this was ridiculous, untrue, and that I could trust Him. God had brought me through several very tough situations before. But it was how I FELT. That became my battle. What I knew vs. what I felt. My prayers to my God now consisted of only: "Help." I knew I needed it. I was ashamed of my own thoughts and feelings. I wanted to be the one who was like a rock of faith, but I was being challenged to my very core. I was shaken and tested in the deepest way. To feel like you have lost all joy and hope is a devastating feeling.

In spite of my anger and hurt, God did answer my prayer and help me. He still is. There were a few ways this help came. I had some close friends who graciously allowed me to express how I felt and never judged me. They questioned and wondered alongside me. Looking back, this was so important. I knew I could trust them with my deepest feelings, and I knew that they would pray me out of the mess that I felt like I was in. I know others were praying relentlessly too. Brandon also helped me many times (and still does) by reminding me to trust what and WHO I know to be true, not how I felt. He had already practiced this earlier in his life, so now he could help me. After my dad wrote me a letter, there was a turn in my perspective about God, and subsequently, in my grieving process.

Somewhere around the fifth week of dealing with all of this, the Lord started to change my heart and my thoughts. I had felt previously (even though I didn't dare say it out loud) that God was "responsible" for taking Danielle away...but now my thoughts were shifting. True, God could have stopped all this, but perhaps He didn't "order" it. Perhaps He simply "allowed" it. That's when I began to be grateful in a new way that Christ had conquered sin and death. The truth is; He had already done more for me than I deserve.

With this change in thought, I crossed a bridge in my healing. I began to pray again and found compassion from the Lord...because I allowed Him to comfort my heart. I still grieve and cry, but now I recognize when I am crossing into despair. Those are the times I need to grab hope from God's Word. I can sing again at church, even though tears usually accompany me. Sometimes, I picture my children and myself before God's throne singing praises together, and I love to read and think about Heaven.

Grief has a way of challenging you and bringing out the very worst. I have felt God's grace deeply, and I am so thankful for it. My perspective on life has changed. My life...Dani Grace's life...is not for MY purpose. It is to bring glory to Him. I have been amazed to see the ways that God has already used Dani's brief life to impact the lives of so many for good. There will always be a part of my heart that is with my children, but God is and will continue to restore my joy and hope in Him here; while I look forward to the day when I will join them in the glorious Heaven they are experiencing.

Some Personal Advice for Friends Seeking to Comfort
These thoughts came after a friend asked me how to help someone going through a similar situation.

<u>Things that were helpful</u>

1. Loving my child -- calling her by name in conversation; not being afraid to talk about her, doing things (or giving me things) in her memory, etc. *(This still means the most.)*

2. Friends who did not correct me or immediately give advice at first, but rather prayed for me or with me.

3. Texting me every day or coming by (always after they asked) to let me know they were thinking of me.

4. Applauding me for making it through another day or big event. This really was a victory at the beginning.

5. Taking me out of the house when I was recovering physically. This helped my mental state.

6. Coming to sit with me (and discussing other topics – not just my grief) so I was not alone during the first several weeks

7. Remembering important dates: for example: Mondays, since they marked another week without Danielle, then the 24th of the month, her due date, etc.

8. Reminding me that the way I choose to hold fast to my faith was honoring the Lord.

9. Overall sensitivity with words and deeds to show compassion.

Things to avoid

I have learned that the way you go about talking with someone who is hurting is important. Grief makes people very sensitive.

1. The casual "How are you?", was something I dreaded for a long time. A simple hug and "I'm praying for you" is better. It is meant well, but putting a grieving person in the position of explaining how they are struggling isn't helpful, especially when that question will come from multiple people in the same day.

2. Saying "I understand what you are going through." Everyone's situation is different. If you want to convey that you have gone through similar grief, say instead; "I know that everyone's situation is unique, but I do remember the feeling of grief from my circumstance."

3. Dictating, not suggesting, what might be of help to the person. For instance, "You need to read this book" or "Go to counseling." Rather, say something like; "When you are ready, you might consider…" I was aware of what I could handle emotionally and sometimes that dictating advice, though heartfelt, was not really helpful.

4. Saying; "God has a reason." This implied to me that God caused the situation, which is not always the case. Say instead, "God will use this." (Romans 8:28)

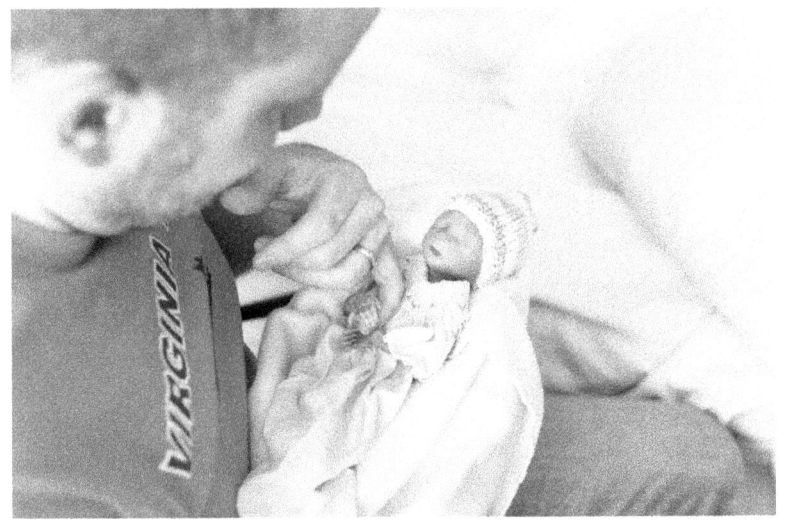

Brandon and Danielle

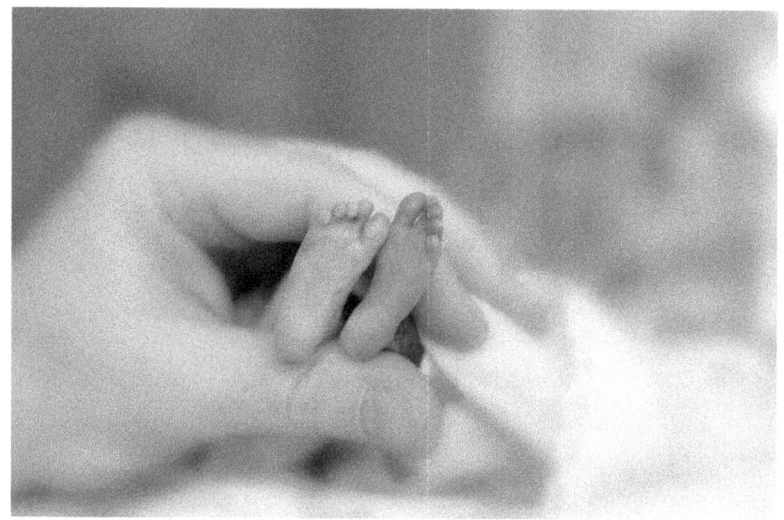

Danielle's little feet

Brandon's Personal Testimony

A Blog post written by Brandon on November 7, 2013:

"You are I AM"

MarySusan said I could write the post tonight. I figured I'd better take the opportunity while I could, considering how often she's been changing her mind about things here lately.

"You Are I AM" by MercyMe. That's the song that was playing on the radio as I got in my car and drove to today's ultrasound. I've heard that song many times, but today I really listened to the lyrics and what it was talking about...

"I've been the one to shake with fear
And wonder if You're even here
I've been the one to doubt Your love
I've told myself You're not enough"

That sounded familiar. I've definitely been there. These last few years have taken their toll. I was the one that trumpeted the fact that God did work a miracle with the first pregnancy in saving MarySusan and keeping her body intact so that we would be able to have kids in the future. I KNEW God was going to let us have our own kids. It was so obvious to me. So we were a little scared, but we knew it was going to be ok...

"I've been the one to try and say
I'll overcome by my own strength
I've been the one to fall apart
And start to question who You are"

But the years went by.....and the disappointment seemed to become an endless cycle. We would see the doctor, our hopes would be skyhigh for two weeks; we'd take a test and have our dreams shattered (again), then we'd just have to wait a few weeks to go see the doctor again....and start over. I started questioning who WAS God?? Was He really concerned with what we were going through?? Had He forgotten what He was supposed to do?? Sure, I looked ok on the outside..... but I had these doubts all the time...

> I've been the one held down in chains
> Beneath the weight of all my shame
> I've been the one to believe
> That where I am You cannot reach"

By this point, I'm thinking it has to be something I'm doing wrong. I'm not having enough faith...I'm not praying the right way....I'm not asking for the right things....I'm just too far gone. I knew my heart, and while I was the one each and every month that told MarySusan it was going to be ok and we'd get it next month, I didn't believe it myself. I was discouraged and believed that I was just misunderstanding God three years ago when I "KNEW" He was going to give us children. I was too far gone and He wasn't going to bless us now. It was too late....

> "You're the one who conquers giants You're the one
> who calls out kings You shut the mouths of lions
> You tell the dead to breathe
> You're the one who walks through fire You take the
> orphan's hand

You are the one Messiah
You are I AM"

Today, I listened to this song and I knew: God IS. That's it. That's what the name "I AM" means. God just IS. Period. End of story. No matter what happens, what we're going through, or what may be coming down the road; God IS. I know it's easier for me to write this now that we're expecting our baby, but that doesn't change God. He still IS. If we lost this baby tomorrow, as hard as that would be, and as many times as I might fail; God. IS. That's just awesome.

A Blog post written by Brandon on March 24, 2014

Danielle Grace – The Journey Continues

Yes, I know.....it has been a LONG time since we have posted anything. We got sidetracked by a lot of excitement.....and a lot of disappointment. A LOT has happened since our last post, so this one may be a little lengthy...

> Hebrews 11:1 says; "Now faith is the sub
> stance of things hoped for, the evidence
> of things not seen."

Things "hoped for" things "not seen".....this is the essence of faith. If we could see and understand everything, there wouldn't be a need for faith. We can't stop blogging about our "Journey of Faith" just because the journey didn't take us where we thought we were going. This is a JOURNEY, not a destination.

One month ago today, MarySusan was rushed to the hospital for abdominal pain. To make a long story not as long, she had serious internal bleeding and had lost a lot of blood already. They rushed her into surgery and while she was on the table, her uterus ruptured and out came our little Danielle Grace. MarySusan started hemorrhaging even more blood, but thankfully they were prepared and ready to save her life. The doctor told me later that if she had not already been on the surgical table and cut open when that happened, she would have bled to death in seconds and they would not have been able to save her. If we had been twenty minutes later getting her into surgery; she wouldn't be here today. I thank God for His perfect timing that we were where we needed to be when that happened.

As most of you know; we lost Danielle that day. Well, we didn't "lose" her....she was God's to give to us and God's to take away. She just got to go home a lot sooner than expected. She got to skip all the pain and heartache of this world, and go straight to be with God. She is safe and filled with peace. I think our best friends' 3-year old boy said it best. When they told him the news, he breathed a huge sigh of relief and said; "I'm happy because Uhfwoppy (what he called her) is with Jesus now and she is happy!'" (He later went on to explain that it was because she got too cramped inside MarySusan, so she had more room with Jesus.) God is good. In the days to follow, we got to hold our little girl over and over again. That was the most AMAZING feeling I have ever experienced and I wouldn't trade it for the world.

So what happened? Didn't I tell the world that Danielle was God's miracle from what happened 3 years ago? Wasn't she supposed to be the testimony of God's grace? Wasn't she supposed to be the evidence of God's working in our lives? I posted all about God being the "I AM" and being a God of miracles. Did He mess up? Did He forget what He was supposed to be doing? No. He didn't.

See, she IS a little miracle.....a miracle we got to hold and kiss and feel. A miracle who has impacted our lives and hearts forever. She is a testimony of God's grace.....God granted us the most amazing 22 weeks and 2 days with this little wonder. She is still evidence of God working in our lives......every single day God is using her to impact not only us, but so many people all over the world. She has had more impact on more people in her few short weeks, than most of us have in our entire lives. My father-in-law was able to lead two people to the Lord who were going through a similar situation at around the same time. God used Dani Grace and our story to touch their hearts and bring them to Himself. Now one day, they will be able to meet the little girl whose short life had such an impact on them! God is still I AM. None of that has changed. God is still God; even if we can't make sense of it all. Now...... before you go all, "Wow Brandon, you have such great faith..." I don't. This concept is a daily...even HOURLY struggle for me. Because I don't get it....I really don't understand. I don't have a clue what God is planning.

I've been reminded of something that a close friend of ours drilled into our head several years ago. Sometimes when life doesn't make sense and you don't understand what God is doing; you just have to KNOW what you KNOW. I don't FEEL like God is faithful, but I KNOW He is. I don't FEEL like God is loving me right now, but I KNOW He does. I don't FEEL like God has remembered what we're going through, but I KNOW He cares. I don't FEEL like God has a plan for us, but I KNOW He does. Faith isn't based on FEELings.... sometimes you just have to KNOW what you KNOW.

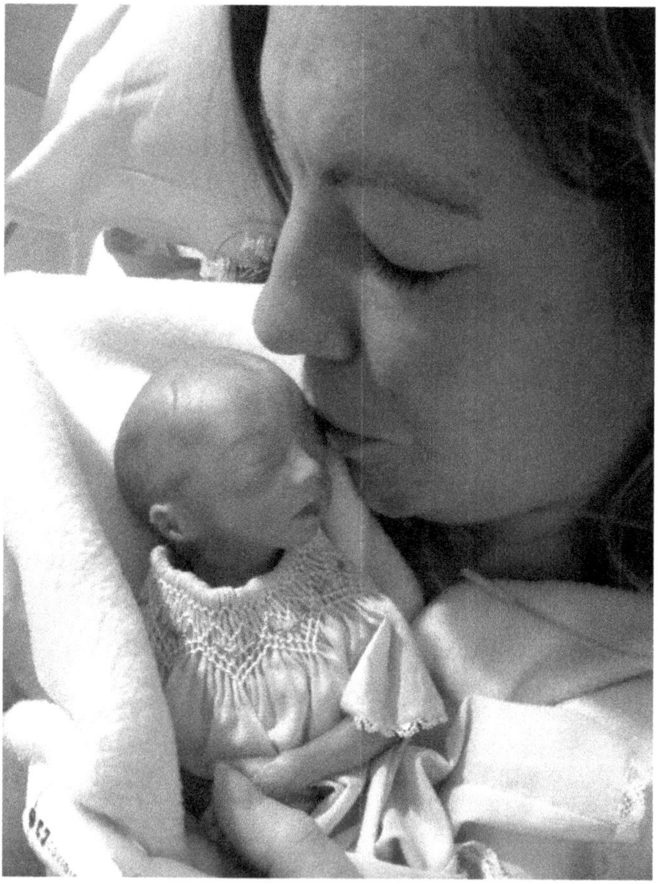

MarySusan embracing Danielle

CHAPTER FOUR

A REASON FOR HOPE

Did you observe the expressions of hope on the part of both Brandon and MarySusan in their tes timonials given in the previous chapter? How is that possible? Some couples seem to never climb out of the dark cellar of despair to see the light of day. Are you one of those who seems to be going through the motions of life, yet far from being able to say in your grief; "See you soon" and mean it with all of your heart?

God's miracle in conception

One of the reasons they, and other Christians who believe the Bible, can have such genuine hope in the midst of suffering is because God's purpose for Danielle was not nullified by her death. God creates a human body in the womb of the mother. While fertilization of that first cell involves both a mom and a dad, it is God who gives a human spirit to indwell the body for the purpose of being able to enjoy life through the senses of the body. Human life is more than the body! Humans are made in the image of God! King David marveled at the role of God in his own development while still in the womb of his mother.

> Psalm 139:16-17; *Thine eyes did see my substance, yet being unperfect; and in thy book all my members were written, which in continuance were fashioned, when as yet there was none of them. How precious also are thy thoughts unto me, O God! How great is the sum of them!*

God's promise even in death

So where is Dani Grace today? She is in the presence of the Lord who created her. When <u>Jesus</u> was on the earth, some little children wanted to come to him. His disciples tried to restrain them from bothering Jesus. This is when Jesus said the following...

> *...Suffer [or permit] the little children to come unto me, and forbid them not: for of such is the kingdom of God,(Mark 10:14)*

If these little children were to have died at that moment, they would have experienced God's blessing in Heaven, not cursing.

> *And he [Jesus] took them up in his arms, and put his hands upon them, and blessed them. (Mark 10:16)*

Someone might ask, "Then why tell little children the Gospel if they don't need to be saved from eternal punishment should they die?" The answer is simple. Share with them the good news of Jesus Christ and his death on the cross for their sins, in order that they might receive him as their personal Lord and Savior before they reach the age of accountability in the sight of God and die in their sins. Ask them to accept Jesus as their personal Savior before they become hardened against God through their own sins for which they later become accountable.

King David had an adulterous relationship with another man's wife, and conspired to have her husband killed in battle when she informed him that she was pregnant with his son. Even though he confessed nine months later in genuine repentance and sorrow for his sin (as recorded in Psalm 51), and the Lord forgave him, there was still some negative consequences he had to suffer as God's chastisement for his sin.

One of those negative consequences was the death of the son who would be born. As the baby was dying, King David refused to eat for seven days and prayed flat on his face before the Lord for God's mercy. The servants were afraid to approach him about any matter during this time, lest he in react in anger. When the baby died, they were afraid to give him the bad news. Upon hearing their whispering, King David asked; "Is the child dead?" When his servants answered in the affirmative, King David arose, bathed, changed his apparel, worshipped the Lord at the Tabernacle, and returned to his palace to eat.

His servants could not understand David's behavior. They asked-

> *What thing is this that thou hast done? Thou didst fast and weep for the child while it was alive; but when the child was dead, thou didst rise and eat bread. (2 Samuel 12:21)*

To which King David responded-

> *While the child was yet alive, I fasted and wept: for I said, Who can tell whether God will be gracious to me, that the child may live? But now he is dead, wherefore should I fast? Can I bring him back again? I shall go to him, but he shall not return to me. (2 Samuel 12:22-23)*

The time for praying and fasting was over. God had not answered King David's prayer in the way that he had desired. But King David still took comfort in the realization that he would be reunited with his son after death.

The apostle Paul wrote that God has prepared a spiritual body in Heaven to clothe the human spirit when it leaves this body here on Earth. A spiritual body is still a body, but it is not made from the ground of this Earth, and it does not depend upon blood to live. Dani Grace woke up in Heaven to enjoy her environment up there, just as she would have enjoyed life here on Earth. It is for this reason that Paul declares that he would rather be absent from this body and present with the Lord.

For we know that if our earthly house of this tabernacle [or body in which our human spirit is presently clothed] *were dissolved* [or returned back to the ground from which it was originally made], *we have a building of God* [another spiritual body that cannot be dissolved], *an house not made with hands* [only God's], *eternal in the heavens* [in which we will never suffer death again]. *For in this we groan, earnestly desiring to be clothed upon with our house which is from heaven: If*

so be that being clothed we shall not be found naked.
(2 Corinthians 5:1-3)

We know Paul is referring to our body in Heaven, and not our current body, for two reasons. First, because he says the purpose is to not be found naked or unclothed when our spirit leaves our current body, and second, because he says he would rather be absent from his earthly body at the time he was writing to be present with the Lord.

> *We are confident, I say, and willing rather to be absent from the body, and to be present with the Lord. (2 Corinthians 5:8)*

The experience in Heaven is so real, that the apostle Paul says he could not tell whether he was in his body or not when he was taken into Heaven to receive special revelation from God. He was so humbled by this experience that he couldn't refer to himself personally when writing about it, lest others think that he was bragging.

> *It is not expedient for me doubtless to glory [or to boast], I will come to visions and revelations of the Lord. I knew a man in Christ above fourteen years ago, (whether in the body, I cannot tell; or whether out of the body, I cannot tell; God knoweth;) such an one caught up to the third heaven. (2 Corinthians 12:1-2)*

So where did Danielle go, according to King David, according to the apostle Paul, and according to the Lord Jesus himself? Where do all babies go when they die? According to the Word of God, they return to the Lord who created them.

The Good News for Dani Grace's Parents

<u>There is another reason</u> Brandon and MarySusan have experienced hope in the midst of sorrow. And that is because they know that they will join Dani Grace in Heaven. This is based upon the Gospel about Jesus, in whom they have believed.

That's what the word "Gospel" means. It is God's Good News about Jesus Christ. A little more than two thousand years ago, Jesus Christ of Nazareth was born. Nazareth was a small town in the land of northern Israel, where Jesus grew as a boy. His was the most unusual birth in all of history, in that he was conceived of God in the womb of the Virgin Mary without having a human father. This was God's way to point him out to the world as the promised divine Son of God whom He would send into the world to save mankind from the eternal penalty of their sins.

In the very first book of the Bible, we are told when death began and why. It happened because the first human couple, Adam and Eve, disobeyed God's command. God had warned them they would die if they disobeyed. If our life comes from God who created us, is it not reasonable for Him to ask for our respect in obeying His commands, especially when those commands are only meant for good from God who gives us life? Yet Adam and Eve sinned, and when they did, their minds were opened to devise their own ideas of right and wrong contrary to the way in which God desires for us to live.

For this reason, God informed Adam and Eve that they would die, and that the bodies He created for them by which to enjoy life would return to the dust from which they were made (Genesis 3:19). The day would come when their human spirit would leave their bodies, and their bodies would return back to the earth.

The reason babies and very young children die is not because of their own sin, but because they are born in the blood line of Adam and Eve, the first sinners. For in their birth, they inherit a nature from Adam to disobey God as did the first parents on this Earth.

> *...in Adam all die. (1 Corinthians 15:22)*

When babies come forth from the womb and grow to become adults, it doesn't take long for them to manifest that they have received this disobedient nature from birth.

> *Wherefore, as by one man [Adam] sin entered into the world, and death by sin; and so death passed upon all men, for that all have sinned. (Romans 5:12)*

> *For all have sinned, and come short of the glory of God. (Romans 3:23)*

Death does not end it all, however, according to the Bible.

> *Hebrews 9:27; And as it is appointed unto men once to die, but after this the judgment.*

The day will come when God will raise all those born in Adam from the dead, and will judge those who lived long enough to become accountable for the sins they expressed against God while in their bodies. But the Good News is this: God promised to send His Son into the world to pay, in His own death on the cross, the penalty we deserve in order that God might save us from His own coming judgment. What love is this!

> John 3:16-17; *For God so loved the world, that he gave his only begotten Son [Jesus, who was born of a woman without a human father], that whosoever believeth in him should not perish, but have everlasting life. For God sent not his Son into the world to condemn the world; but that the world through him might be saved.*

But to be saved, one must believe in the Lord Jesus Christ.

> Acts 16:31; *Believe on the Lord Jesus Christ, and thou shalt be saved and thy house.*

Brandon and MarySusan have obeyed that command. As "*Lord*," they believe Jesus to be God and not just a man; as "*Jesus*," they believe He left Heaven as God's only begotten Son and became human like us in order to die for our sins; and as "*Christ*," they believe that He is alive, having risen from the dead, and is coming again to bring God's kingdom to Earth before He destroys it and creates a new Heaven and a new Earth in which there will be no more sin or death.

Because they have believed this in their hearts; Brandon and MarySusan have also obeyed the command to express their faith personally to God, by calling upon the name of the Lord Jesus for their eternal forgiveness and salvation.

> Romans 10:9, 13; *That if thou shalt confess with thy mouth the Lord Jesus, and shalt believe in thine heart that God hath raised him from the dead, thou shalt be saved... For whosoever shall call upon the name of the Lord shall be saved.*

Have you done this, dear reader? Danielle did not reach an age to sin against God with her mind, heart, or body. She is therefore not accountable to God. But you are, and you know it down deep in the secrets of your own heart. Being accountable, there is no one else God has provided for you whereby you can be eternally saved and forgiven by God who made you.

> John 14:6; *Jesus saith unto him, I am the way, the truth, and the life: no man cometh unto the Father, but by me.*

> Acts 4:12; *Neither is there salvation in any other; for there is none other name under heaven given among men, whereby we must be saved.*

It is because Brandon and MarySusan have heard the Gospel and put their trust for salvation in God's divine Son, the Lord Jesus, and in Him alone, that they can have hope in the midst of sorrow. That they can say with heartfelt belief and confidence in God and His promises; "See You Soon!"

These promises are for you, regardless of who you are or where you live. Turn to Jesus Christ for your salvation and comfort, and you will be able to enjoy God's promise for you today, right now!

John 5:24; *Verily, Verily [you can count on this], I say unto you [Jesus, when he lived on this earth in Israel], He that heareth my word [now, in this life], and believeth on him that sent me [his Heavenly Father], hath everlasting life [already], and shall not come into condemnation, but is passed from death unto life.*

If you would like more information about the Lord Jesus Christ, please see the contact information at the beginning of the book.

CHAPTER FIVE

DEALING WITH SORROW

The following words of advice are for those who are Christians. Until a person has accepted Jesus Christ as his or her personal Savior, he remains separated from God. He is therefore unable to receive God's comfort in the midst of great grief. Read Chapter Four if you are not sure of your relationship to God through Jesus Christ.

When Grief Becomes Harmful

When the storm of a tragedy hits, understand what usually happens emotionally. Fear will enter your heart. This is a part of life. You cannot help it. Waves of sorrow will seem to overwhelm you any time your mind thinks about it, causing the tears to flow and the heart to ache. The Psalmist cries out when being separated from his acquaintance with the following words: *Psa.88:9; Mine eye mourneth by reason of affliction.*

Understand the potential devastating effect. Satan seizes the opportunity to destroy the usefulness of the believer when he is down. He seeks to intensify the sorrow and make the emotional pain so intense that the believer will be crushed in spirit.

Prolonged intense heartache or grief can lead to psychological depression, physical depression, and illness. Proverbs 13:12; *Hope deferred maketh the heart sick: but when the desire cometh, it is a tree of life.* Proverbs 15:13; *A merry heart maketh a cheerful countenance: but by sorrow of the heart the spirit is broken.*

The end result could be a sense of hopelessness that could lead to suicidal thoughts. The apostle Peter reminded his readers to cast their burdens upon the Lord, for *he careth for you.* (1 Peter 5:7) The reason he did so, is because there is an enemy of the believer who does not care. Rather, he –like a roaring lion – seeks whom *he may devour*, or destroy. (1 Pet.5:8)

Understand as well, how to keep from being overwhelmed when under emotional attack. It is healthy to grieve, to shed tears. But recognize the moment any feelings of fear and despair enter your heart in the grieving process, and immediately counter them with the shield of faith.

Paul says that the believer needs to put on the *whole armor of God*, which includes the *shield of faith* whereby the believer can quench all the *fiery darts of the wicked.* (Eph.6:16) The Psalmist wrote; *What time I am afraid, I will trust in thee* (Psalm 56:3) Notice, it is at the time or the moment one feels afraid, that he is to counter that fear with faith in the Lord!

How to put up the Shield of Faith:

First, <u>focus your thoughts upon Christ</u> and His understanding compassion for you. After all, Jesus left heaven to become a man, and suffered rejection. He *came unto his own, and his own received him not.* (John 1:11) He was a man who was *despised and rejected of men; a man of sorrows, and acquainted with grief.* Yet He not only bore his own sorrow, but took upon himself to bear the sorrows of the world because of sin. *He "bore "our griefs, and carried our sorrows: yet we did esteem him stricken, smitten of God and afflicted. But he was wounded for our transgressions, he was bruised for our iniquities: the chastisement of our peace was upon him: and which his stripes we are healed.* (Isaiah 53:3-5)

When Jesus sent His disciples ahead in a ship on the Sea of Galilee, a storm arose threatening their lives. Jesus, who Himself had been praying, walked on the water to go out to them. The disciples cried out for fear when they saw Him, thinking Him to be a ghost. Jesus then spoke to them, saying, *Be of good cheer: it is I, be not afraid.* Jesus wanted His disciples to learn to keep their eyes upon Him in the storms of life.

Peter at first, went to Jesus, walking on water, but when he saw the boisterous winds, *<u>he was afraid</u>; and beginning to sink, he cried, saying, Lord, save me.* Jesus immediately held out his hand and saved Peter from drowning, asking him why he doubted. When they came into the boat, the storm ceased and the disciples worshipped him, saying *Of a truth, thou art the Son of God.* (Matthew 14:22-33)

In another instance, Jairus, a ruler of the synagogue, came to Jesus urging him to come down to his house to heal his daughter who was about to die. Jesus said he would come, but on the way was sidetracked by another woman with an issue of blood. After healing her, Jesus heard certain ones inform Jairus that his daughter had died. There was no use troubling Jesus over the matter anymore. Jesus knew the fear and sorrow that would immediately enter the heart of this father, and so the Scripture records that *as soon as Jesus heard the word that was spoken, he saith unto the ruler of the synagogue, <u>Be not afraid, only believe.</u>*

Second, <u>cry out to God in believing prayer</u>, reciting His promises out loud if possible. <u>Keep doing so until you feel the strength of God rise up within to help deaden the pain.</u> *Hear my cry, O God: attend unto my prayer. From the end of the earth will <u>I cry unto thee, when my heart is overwhelmed</u>: lead me to the rock that is higher than I.* (Psalm 61:1-2)

> Psalm 62:5-8; *My soul, wait thou only upon God, for my expectation is from him. He only is my rock and my salvation: he is my defence; I shall not be moved. In God is my salvation, and my glory; <u>the rock of my strength</u>, and my refuge, is in God. Trust in him at all times: ye people, <u>pour out your heart before him</u>: God is a refuge for us. Selah.*

> Philippians 4:6-7; *Be careful for nothing (or anxious about anything): but in everything by prayer and supplication (petition for grace) with thanksgiving let your requests be made known unto God. And <u>the peace of God, which passeth all understanding</u>, shall keep your hearts and minds through Christ Jesus.*

Third, <u>give thanks to God</u> when He answers your prayer for inner strength. *In every thing give thanks: for this* [the giving of thanks in everything] *is the will of God in Christ Jesus concerning you.* (1 Thessalonians 5:18)

<u>Be on the Alert</u>

One never knows when he or she is vulnerable to sudden emotional attack. For example, a key time is when you are alone. Memories of the way things were before the tragedy hit deepens the heartache. Try to minimize such times of being alone as much as possible while healing emotionally. Even when you are not alone, something you see, or something you hear, might contribute to more heartache. Avoid these triggers if possible while you are healing.

At night, Satan will attack you while you are sleeping, causing you to awake from a nightmare with pain in your heart. You will awaken to feelings of emptiness, fear, and sadness. Immediately put up your shield of faith in prayer, focusing upon the Lord and the promises of Scripture. Reading His promises immediately before going to sleep can help prevent these attacks.

Intensify your efforts to prepare yourself for any future attacks. When you are alone is the time to read God's promises out loud to the Lord in prayer before any attack comes. Do not allow your mind to focus upon the sorrow. Focus upon Christ by thinking of who He is, why He came to Earth, what He did when He was on Earth, where He is now, what He is doing for you now, and what He promises to do for you in the future.

Pray for yourself the prayer Paul wrote for the Ephesian believers in Ephesians 3:14-21. Remember as well what he wrote to the Philippian believers;

Rejoice in the Lord always, and again I say, rejoice. (Phil.4:4)

Do Not Make Matters Worse

Do not allow Satan to wound your heart any more than it is already by trying to handle the problem in your own strength. Jesus knew His disciples were sorrowful that He was about to depart from them and go to His Heavenly Father. The reason they did not ask Him where He was going, is because sorrow had filled their hearts. (John 16:6)

This is why Jesus told them in the very next verse that it was necessary that He send to them the Holy Spirit after His departure in order to comfort them in their separation from Him. So it is one of the purposes of the Holy Spirit, who comes to indwell every believer today, to be of help and comfort until Jesus comes back to receive us unto Himself.

It is vital therefore, that we not quench the Holy Spirit, so that He can come to our aid in times of trouble and sorrow. (1 Thes. 5:19)

Another way in which we can make matters worse is by responding to such heartache by wallowing in feelings of self-pity and anger. This is sinful and quenches any comfort the Holy Spirit might provide to offset the heartache.

> Ephesians 5:30-31; *And grieve not the holy Spirit of God, whereby ye are sealed unto the day of redemption. Let all bitterness, and wrath, and anger, and clamour, and evil speaking be put away from you, with all malice: And be ye kind*

one to another, tenderhearted, forgiving one another, even as God for Christ's sake hath forgiven you.

Worrying over how the problem will be resolved and when the heartache will go away does not help, but rather compounds the hurt. Do not try to change what you have no control over. Worrying only opens the door for Satan to intensify the emotional stress. Read again the Scriptures above; Phillipians 4:6-7 and 1 Peter 5:7-8. Live by faith, taking it one day at a time. (Matthew 6:34)

Discipline your mind to think Biblically, not negatively

Phil.4:8; *Finally, brethren, whatsoever things are true, whatsoever things are honest, whatsoever things are just, whatsoever things are pure, whatsoever things are lovely, whatsoever things are of good report; if there be any virtue, and if there be any praise, think on these things..*

Seek to be around Christians who will help you to think this way. *Those things which ye have both learned, and received, and heard, and seen in me, do: and the God of peace shall be with you.* (Phi.4:9) The apostle Paul described his ministry as *sorrowful, yet always rejoicing.* (2 Corinthians 6:10)

Claim the promise of Romans 8:28; *And we know that all things work together for good to them that love God, to them who are the called according to his purpose.*

If these simple rules are followed, the heartache will subside, the joy of life will return, and you will remain tender in your heart towards the Lord, towards people, and towards life in general. You will then be able to comfort others in sorrow with the comfort by which God sustained you.

> 2 Corinthians 3-4; *Blessed be God, even the Father of our Lord Jesus Christ, the Father of mercies, and the God of all comfort; Who comforteth us in all our tribulation, that we may be able to comfort them which are in any trouble, by the comfort wherewith we ourselves are comforted by God.*

Some Verses to Pray

Here are some verses to cry out to God immediately when under an emotional, panic attack. Keep doing this until the attack subsides.

From the Book of Psalms

> *The Lord also will be a refuge for the oppressed, a refuge in times of trouble. And they that know thy name will put their trust in thee: for thou Lord hast not forsaken them that seek thee.* (9:9-10)

> *I will love thee, O Lord, my strength. The Lord is my rock, and my fortress, and my deliverer; my God, my strength, in whom I will trust: my buckler, and the horn of my salvation, and my high tower.* (18:1-2)

> *In my distress I called upon the Lord, and cried unto my God; he heard my voice out*

of his temple, and my cry came before him, even into his ears. (18:6)

The Lord hear thee in the day of trouble. The name of the God of Jacob defend thee: Send thee help from the sanctuary, and strengthen thee out of Zion. (20:1-2)

The Lord is my light and my salvation; whom shall I fear? The Lord is the strength of my life; of whom shall I be afraid? (27:1)

Hear, O Lord, when I cry with my voice: have mercy also upon me, and answer me. When thou saidst, Seek ye my face; my heart said unto thee, Thy face, Lord, will I seek. (27:7-8)

I had fainted, unless I had believed to see the goodness of the Lord in the land of the living. Wait on the Lord: be of good courage, and he shall strengthen thine heart: wait, I say, on the Lord. (27:13-14)

Blessed be the Lord, because he hath heard the voice of my supplications. The Lord is my strength and my shield; my heart trusted in him, and I am helped: therefore my heart greatly rejoiceth; and with my song will I praise him. (28:6-7)

Be of good courage, and he shall strengthen your heart, all ye that hope in the Lord. (31:24)

I will bless the Lord at all times: his praise shall continually be in my mouth. My soul shall make her boast in the Lord: the humble shall hear thereof, and be glad. O magnify the Lord with me, and let us exalt his name together. (34:1-6)

I sought the Lord, and he heard me, and delivered me from all my fears. They looked unto him, and were lightened: and their faces were not ashamed. This poor man cried, and the Lord heard him, and saved him out of all his troubles. The eyes of the Lord are upon the righteous, and his ears are open unto their cry. (34:15)

The righteous cry, and the Lord heareth, and delivereth them out of all their troubles. The Lord is nigh unto them that are of a broken heart: and saveth such as be of a contrite spirit. Many are the afflictions of the righteous: but the Lord delivereth him out of them all. (34:17-19)

The Lord redeemeth the soul of his servants: and none of them that trust in him shall be desolate. (34:22)

Why art thou cast down, O my soul? And why art thou disquieted in me? Hope thou in God: for I shall yet praise him for the help of his countenance. (34:5)

God is our refuge and strength, a very present help in trouble. (46:1)

And call upon me in the day of trouble: I will deliver thee, and thou shalt glorify me. (50:15)

Cast thy burden upon the Lord, and he shall sustain thee: he shall never suffer the righteous to be moved. (55:22)

Evening, and morning, and at noon, will I pray, and cry aloud: and he shall hear my voice. (55:17)

What time I am afraid, I will trust in thee. In God I will praise his word, in God I have put my trust; I will not fear what flesh can do unto me. (56:3-4)

Be merciful unto me, O God, be merciful unto me: for my soul trusteth in thee: yea, in the shadow of thy wings will I make my refuge, until these calamities be overpast. (57:1)

Hear my cry, O God; attend unto my prayer. From the end of the earth will I cry unto thee, when my heart is overwhelmed: lead me to the rock that is higher than I. (61:1-2)

Truly my soul waiteth upon God: from him cometh my salvation. He only is my rock and my salvation; he is my defence; I shall not be greatly moved. (62:1-2)

Trust in him at all times; ye people, pour out your heart before him: God is a refuge for us. Selah. (62:8)

O God, thou art my God; early will I seek thee: my soul thirsteth for thee, my flesh longeth for thee in a dry and thirsty land, where no water is. (63:1)

Thus will I bless thee while I live: I will lift up my hands in thy name. My soul shall be satisfied as with marrow and fatness; and my mouth shall praise thee with joyful lips: When I remember thee upon my bed, and meditate on thee in the night watches. (63:4-8)

Because thou hast been my help, therefore in the shadow of thy wings will I rejoice. My soul followeth hard after thee: thy right hand upholdeth me. Whom have I in heaven but thee? And there is none upon earth that I desire beside thee. (73:25-26)

My flesh and my heart faileth: but God is the strength of my heart, and my portion forever. But it is good for me to draw near to God: I have put my trust in the Lord God, that I may declare all thy works. (73:28)

I cried unto God with my voice, even unto God with my voice; and he gave ear unto me. (77:1)

For the Lord God is a sun and shield: the Lord will give grace and glory: no good thing will he withhold from them that walk uprightly. O Lord of hosts, blessed is the man that trusteth in thee. (84:11-12)

Bow down thine ear, O Lord, hear me: for I am poor and needy. Preserve my soul; for I am holy: O thou my God, save thy servant that trusteth in thee. Be merciful unto me, O Lord: for I cry unto thee daily. Rejoice the soul of thy servant: for unto thee, O Lord, do I lift up my soul. For thou, Lord, art good, and ready to forgive; and plenteous in mercy unto all them that call upon thee. Give ear, O Lord, unto my prayer; and attend to the voice of my supplications. In the day of my trouble I will call upon thee: for thou wilt answer me. (86:1-7)

Teach my thy way, O Lord; I will walk in thy truth: unite my heart to fear thy name.

I will praise thee, O Lord my God, with all my heart: and I will glorify thy name forevermore. (86:11-12)

O Lord God of my salvation, I have cried day and night before thee: Let my prayer come before thee: incline thine ear unto my cry. (88:1-2)

He that dwelleth in the secret place of the most High shall abide under the shadow of the Almighty. I will say of the Lord, He is my refuge and my fortress: my God; in him will I trust. (91:1-2)

Because he hath set his love upon me, therefore will I deliver him: I will set him on high, because he hath known my name. He shall call upon me, and I will answer him: I will be with him in trouble; I will deliver him, and honour him. With long life will I satisfy him, and shew him my salvation. (91:14-16)

Unless the Lord had been my help, my soul had almost dwelt in silence. When I said, My foot slippeth; thy mercy O Lord, held me up. In the multitude of my thoughts within me thy comforts delight my soul. (94:17-19)

Hear my prayer, O Lord, and let my cry come unto thee. Hide not thy face from me in the day when I am in trouble; incline thine ear unto me: in the day when I call answer me speedily. (102:1)

He will regard the prayer of the destitute, and not despise their prayer. This shall be written for the generation to come: and the people which shall be created shall praise the Lord. (102:17-18)

Seek the Lord, and his strength: seek his face evermore. (105:4)

Help me, O Lord my God: O save me according to thy mercy: That they may know that this is thy hand; that thou, Lord has done it. (109:26-27)

I love the Lord, because he hath heard my voice and my supplication.

Because he hath inclined his ear unto me, therefore will I call upon him as long as I live. (116:1-2)

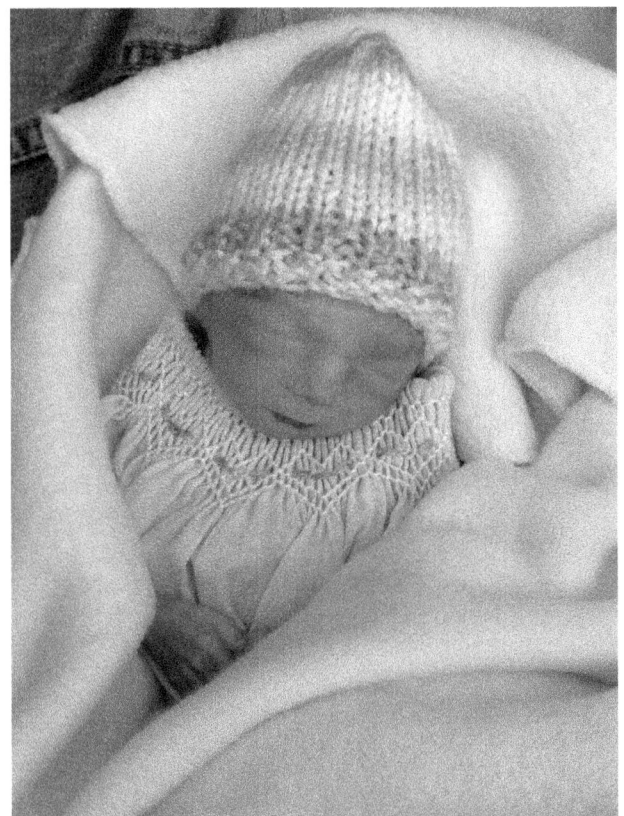

Dani Grace

CHAPTER SIX
FINAL TRIBUTES

FROM DANI GRACE TO MOMMY
(Letter written by Brandon to MarySusan on Mother's Day)

May 11, 2014

Hi Mommy,

We just wanted to wish you a very Happy Mother's Day! We wish we could have been there to celebrate with you today, but we are going to have to wait a little bit longer before we get to see you again. We heard that you had a pretty good day and are so glad you were able to be recognized as a "real" mother.....because you are, and always will be, OUR mother.

You have had the heart of a mother for as long as you can remember, always longing for the day when you could hold us. We would have been the luckiest kids on earth to have been able to grow up in your loving arms. We would have loved to be able to wake you up early on a Saturday morning running through the house chasing each other. I would have totally blamed it on my older sibling....because it definitely would have been their fault. We wish we could learn to make pancakes and eggs from you...even if it might not have been pretty. :)

We would have loved for you to come to our soccer games and cheerleading competitions....you would have been so proud of us. We miss that we will not be able to talk to you and ask advice through our teenage years.....and then run into your loving arms after we do the opposite of what you tell us to. We wish we could have shared the experience of our first loves....and first broken hearts with you. We know you would have let us cry on your shoulder and reassure us that our world was not ending. We will miss getting to see the look on your face as we bring home the "special someones" to meet you and daddy.....and then watching as you tell dad to put away his gun. We wish we would be able to share that special day as we commit our lives to someone forever. We know you would have been so happy and proud of us......because we would have picked partners just like you and daddy.

There are a lifetime of memories that we will miss out on, but that's ok....it's only a lifetime. When you get up here, we will have FOREVER to make memories.....but right now, God has something else for you to do. He has some other plan for you. Somewhere, someday, there are some kids out there that He needs you to be a mom to. And that's ok....we're willing to share.... because we know that those kids are going to be the luckiest kids ever to walk the face of the earth. You are one AMAZING person and we are so lucky to be able to call you....MOM. We love you and are counting the days until we see you again....

Love,

Dani Grace and Baby # 1

Blog post written on the due date of Danielle by MarySusan

June 28, 2014

The tears start almost the second I open my eyes. Why am I surprised by this? After all, shouldn't I be crying since today is the day that represents what should have been? A day filled with joy at the arrival of our little girl. But instead life tends to be a bit of a fight now. I mean a real battle of my emotions, which this week I felt like I had been conquering for the most part. I get tired of crying, and knowing that this day was approaching; I had been fighting for some sense of joy and normalcy all week.

However, this morning I didn't want to even get out of bed. But I got up anyway. Because I knew I had to. Whether she can really see me or not, I want my little girl to be proud of her Mommy. So I get up. For her. I choose to keep going, not because I really have a strong desire to seize the days or face the world, but I have to choose to take steps forward. Today that meant starting by getting up. More than grief, I want to cele-brate and honor Dani's little life. I want others to as well.

I look at my Bible app and Psalm 23 appears from where I had been reading last night. "Yea, though I walk through the valley of the shadow of death, I will fear no evil; for You are with me..." Even though I may not be the one facing death, I am certainly affected by it now. And God's Word reminds me that He is with me. My sweet husband texts me reminding me that he loves me and we are in this together. What would I do without him? Next, the doorbell rings. Beautiful flowers are waiting. From a sweet friend who remembers Dani's life often and isn't afraid to talk about her. This isn't the first time in this journey that God has used others to encourage me to keep going.

So, even though the tears flow continuously like rain (and I know that's okay), I try to think of what I can do for my baby. I have found that it helps me to find things to do FOR her. I pull out her baby book and work on finishing it...something I haven't had the courage to do up to this point. Later we will get fresh flowers and visit her grave. (I am thankful in a strange way for this spot to go to. I know that's not where Danielle really is, but with my first baby I didn't have this.)

God has been gracious this week to give me glimpses of perspective. Reminders of how broken and sinful this awful world is. These last four months, I have understood, felt, and been more grateful than ever that Jesus conquered death. Though I selfishly want Danielle with me every day, if it came right down to it, how could I wish her away from the perfect peace she is enjoying in heaven to come live down here? So instead, I will look forward to the day when I can go join her.

I sit here writing with Danielle's little dress and hospital blanket by me, but also surrounded by other things given to us by special people. Things that were given to show us that they remember and love our Dani too. The sweetest thing that lifts this Mommy's heart is when people talk about my daughter by name. So, yes, please continue to pray for us as walk this road.

We still desperately need it. Thank God with us today for this wonderful blessing named Danielle Grace. God has used her little life so much already and we pray He will continue to.

Dani Grace, you may have a different (and much better) address now, but you are remembered and loved so much! Especially by Mommy and Daddy. Can't wait to see you again, our little Monkey.

A Song Written by Dr. Daniel R. Carfrey "Blessed be the God of All Comfort"

Blessed Be the God of All Comfort

Dr. Daniel R Carfrey

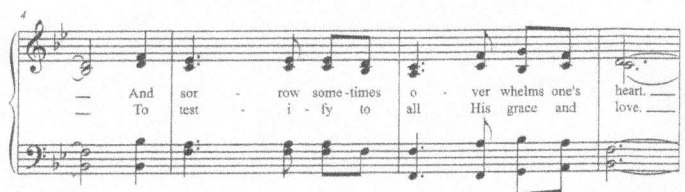

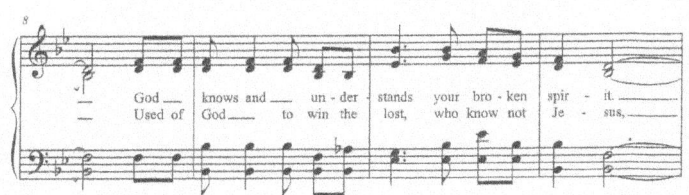

March 7, 2010

Blessed Be the God of All Comfort

Memorial Service For Danielle Grace Williams

Private services at the graveside, Cedar Lawn Memorial Park, Roanoke Virginia

Service Time: 2:00 P.M, Wednesday, March 5, 2014
Officiating: Pastor Robert L. Alderman

Danielle Grace was preceded in death by a sibling in September 2010
Surviving:

> Parents: MarySusan C. Williams & Brandon B. Williams
> Maternal Grandparents: Daniel Carfrey & Shirley Carfrey
> Paternal Grandparents: Leslie Williams & Jean Williams
> Aunts: Holly Williams, Valerie Williams & Emily Davis & Husband John

I want to begin our time together with a particular promise from the Bible.

You will keep Him in perfect peace whose mind is stayed [fixed] *on you, because he trusts in you.* (Isaiah 26:3)

We have all come to a moment in time when we need an infusion of peace. Some of the reasons we gather for a service like this.

— We are bearing each other's burdens
— We are honoring the life of a child, even though that life passed from us so quickly
— We are expressing our love for family and friends and Christian relationships
— We are facing the reality of death with the courage of faith and the power of togetherness
— We are rejoicing in life while mourning the sadness of death

We are rejoicing in the promises of resurrection and eternal life for children.

— We get this reality even before the time of our Lord's resurrection. It was the King of Israel who said of his deceased child – *I shall go to him, but he shall not return to me.* (2 Samuel 12:23)

We are rejoicing in the invitation and promise of our Lord with reference to children.

— *But Jesus said, Suffer little children, and forbid them not to come unto me: for of such is the kingdom of heaven.* (Matthew 19:14)

70

We are rejoicing in the promise of peace.

— *Peace I leave with you, my peace I give unto you: not as the world giveth, give I unto you. Let not your heart be troubled, neither let it be afraid.* (John14:27)

And we are encouraging the value of memory.

— Though Danielle's life here on Earth was short, our gathering is a portion of the memory we will have of her presence and the gift of her life.

www.ingramcontent.com/pod-product-compliance
Lightning Source LLC
Chambersburg PA
CBHW051235120626
46547CB00013B/1656